Help Wanted!

McDougal & Associates
Servants of Christ and stewards of the mysteries of God

Help Wanted!

Vacancies in the Kingdom of God

by

Linda Gourdine-Hunt

Unless otherwise noted, all Scripture references are from The New King James Version of the Bible, copyright © 1979, 1980, 1982, by Thomas Nelson, Inc., Nashville, Tennessee. References marked "KJV" are from the King James Version of the Bible.

Cover design by Sherie Campbell
sonandshield@comcast.net

Published by:

McDougal & Associates
18896 Greenwell Springs Road
Greenwell Springs, LA 70739
www.thepublishedword.com

McDougal & Associates is dedicated to the spreading of the Gospel of Jesus Christ to as many people as possible in the shortest time possible.

ISBN 13: 978-1-934769-24-9
ISBN 10: 1-934769-24-X

Printed in the United States of America
For Worldwide Distribution

Dedication

To my grandmamma, *Helen Capers Scott*, whose light will always shine in my heart.

ACKNOWLEDGMENTS

I humbly acknowledge the invaluable help of the following:

God, for His message, vision and grace that enabled me to do this work for His glory

Steve, my husband, for his prayers, sacrifice, encouragement and loving support throughout this entire assignment

Tareak Johnson, my son, whose support and contributions I will always treasure. I pray that you will continue to allow God to use you for His glory.

Tonya, my beautiful daughter, for your prayers, sensitivity and love.

Kim Moss, my gooood girlfriend of more than twenty-five years who has been encouraging me to do this work for the past fifteen of those years. Thank you for your ideas, persistence and labor of love. Most of all, thank you for being you.

McDougal & Associates, my publishers. I'm grateful. Thank you.

Labeebah Matheen, my faithful sister since 1972. Thank you for your love and encouragement throughout the years.

Special thanks to all of you who contributed to the section "Others Share" and a special shout-out to all family, friends, associates and co-workers who helped in any and every way. May God richly bless each and every one of you.

CONTENTS

Then Jesus went about all the cities and villages, teaching in their synagogues, preaching the gospel of the kingdom, and healing every sickness and every disease among the people. But when He saw the multitudes, He was moved with compassion for them, because they were weary and scattered, like sheep having no shepherd. Then He said to His disciples, "The harvest truly is plentiful, but the laborers are few. Therefore pray the Lord of the harvest to send out laborers into His harvest." Matthew 9:35-38

INTRODUCTION

For years I wondered why I had been born. What was my purpose in life? I often went to bed overwhelmed, especially after watching the evening news. There were so many problems in the world. What could I do to make a difference in the lives of those in need?

At the same time I was (and still am) in utter awe of God. How could He take care of all the people in this vast world? How was He able to answer the cry of a mother whose baby was terminally ill and, at the same time be concerned about the fact that I wanted a veggie pizza or some Utz potato chips to eat? To me, that was so amazing!

Then, through the study of His Word, I learned that God uses people just like me to do His bidding. We are His hands, His feet, His smile and His loving arms in this world. We, to whom He has given gifts without repentance, are the answer to every social ill—from hunger on American Indian reservations to the senseless killings in Darfur, Africa.

The Word of God shows us that Jesus was afflicted in every way that we are all afflicted, and so He feels the pain of all mankind. He knows where we all hurt.

Knowing that He loves us gives us a feeling of comfort—even in the midst of the most difficult trials and tribulations of life. And He delights in delivering us from our distresses. He does this by working through us to meet the needs of others. Suddenly I had a purpose in life.

In the Fall of 1993, I was invited to a service where a prophet was preaching. His message that night was entitled "All I Have Is a Jar of Oil" and was based on the story of the Shunammite woman in the book of Second Kings. It was a life-changing message, one that caused me to take inventory of my own life. It was a season in which physical resources were extremely strained, and yet I discovered that there was a jar of oil within me. God had blessed me with a strong voice, along with writing and speaking abilities. These were gifts that I could use for the advancement of God's Kingdom.

At a subsequent service, God spoke to me again through the same prophet about a message that would go throughout the nation. Not long after that, while sitting in my living room in Jamaica, New York, having a conversation with my Father God, I was inspired to write a flier containing the seeds of the message of this book.

Due in large part to my dear friend and sister Kim B. Moss, who practically dragged me to the print shop, indifferent to my protests, *Help Wanted: A Divine Call from the Heart of God to His People* was soon in print, and I have been blessed ever since to deliver this message to God's people at home and abroad, and as I have done so, the revelation of it has grown.

What gifts did God give you? Can you sing? Can you

write? Maybe you can play an instrument or cook. Can you listen to someone with a broken heart? There is something for every one of us to do. Follow His leading, as He guides you, to reach out and touch someone with a heart of love.

This cry from the heart of God is going out to whosoever will to help better the human condition. If you have compassion and a heart full of desire to use the gifts He has given you, then please consider His invitation.

Jesus Christ is the greatest employer you could ever have, and there is plenty of work to be done in His Kingdom. He said, *"The harvest truly is plentiful, but the laborers are few"* (Matthew 9:37). I have answered His ad. Will you join me today?

Linda Gourdine-Hunt
Springfield Gardens, New York

Part I

Help Wanted!

CLASSIFIEDS

VACANCIES

Seeking full-time and part-time positions for:

STREET★MINISTERS

Positions to be filled wherever the homeless and hungry reside. Must be a people person, willing to serve with love and compassion. Knowledge of the Word of God required to pray, encourage and comfort those in need. Knowledge of community resources also helpful.

Excellent spiritual pay and eternal benefits

CALL: L-O-R-D-S-E-N-D-M-E

* The Kingdom of the Lord Jesus Christ does not discriminate on the basis of race, creed, color, origin or gender.

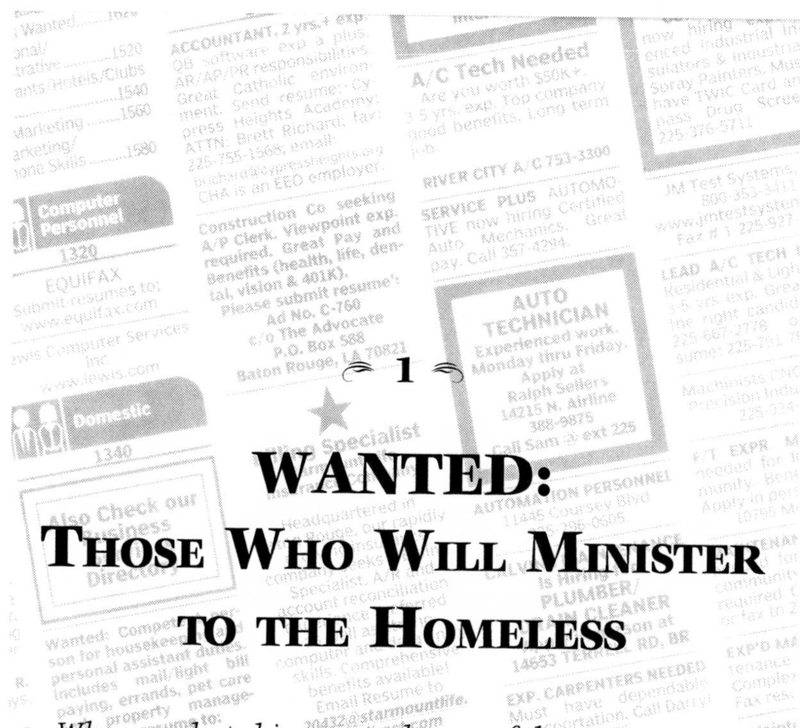

1

WANTED: THOSE WHO WILL MINISTER TO THE HOMELESS

Whoever shuts his ears to the cry of the poor
Will also cry himself and not be heard.

Proverbs 21:13

It's a cool breezy day, when Jesus Christ, our Lord and Savior, decides to leave His throne in Glory to take a casual walk through the vast open fields. You see, it's harvest time, and He wants to survey the fruit of His fields. What do you think He will find?

Under the clear distant skies, He arrives on the shores of the field in time to see Bob, a homeless man, busily engaged in his morning task of sifting through the contents of his neighborhood garbage cans in hopes of finding something to eat.

The Cry of a Homeless Man

With hands outstretched to those who pass by, I plead,
"Please spare some change for a lowly man in need."
Yet, it seems, my pleas fall on peers with deaf ears,
while I walk these streets full of need and wept tears.

To survive when hunger strikes, my pride is subsided,
so the trash that others pass I yearn for what's inside it.
With strength and resolve, I dismiss germs and disease,
and with humility of heart give thanks for the received.

So I close my eyes, and I force to swallow
to silence the cries of my belly's hollow.
With tears, I reminisce of the meals with fine wine.
Now it's dumpsters with discarded meals for the fine dine.

To hide the pain of being greatly reduced,
I hide in the shadows as a homeless recluse.
Will work for food, but denied the hire;
they tell me "instability" and "improper attire."

I try shelters, waiting hours in line,
but the needs of a family are greater than mine.
What can I do that I may rise above this,
to escape the reality of a world so loveless?
To stop and talk, no one dares;

they know the needs, but no one shares.
They know the hurts, but no one cares,
so I know I'm on the lips of no one's prayers.

I'm growing tired, hurt, lonely and weary
of asking for help in a world that won't hear me.
So tonight, when I lay and conclude this day,
in my world where the sun don't shine,
while others pray to be kept in their sleep,
I pray He'll take me in mine.

— Tareak Johnson

WANTED IN THE KINGDOM OF GOD: THOSE WHO WILL MINISTER TO THE HOMELESS!

CLASSIFIEDS

VACANCIES

YOUTH WORKERS NEEDED

Able to counsel pregnant and parenting teens according to the Word of God.
Experience in working with youth and families at risk.
Knowledge of educational and social support systems and resources a must.

Excellent spiritual pay and eternal benefits

CALL: L-O-R-D-S-E-N-D-M-E

* The Kingdom of the Lord Jesus Christ does not discriminate on the basis of race, creed, color, origin or gender.

2

WANTED: THOSE WHO WILL MINISTER TO PREGNANT TEENS

Come to Me, all you who labor and are heavy laden, and I will give you rest. Take My yoke upon you and learn from Me, for I am gentle and lowly in heart, and you will find rest for your souls. Matthew 11:28-29

Moving further into the heart of the field, our Lord sees Lizzie, a sixteen-year-old pregnant teenager. Sitting huddled in a park, lonely and afraid, she thinks of committing suicide, because no one takes the time to talk with her. No one seems to understand.

Pregnant and in Despair

How long will this last, the finger pointing and laughter,
The mistake I made, when in bed I laid,
And the consequences after?

So young, so foolish, my curiosity got the best of me.
They talk and taunt, spread lies and speak the less of me.
My family is embarrassed; they say I caused them shame.
Now they want to disown me, for I've disgraced their name.

I'm scared, lonely, depressed and rejected,
Paying the price for sex unprotected.
How could I be so stupid, to give something so priceless?
He left me alone, to bear this on my own,
Without his help to fight this.

Do I abort and move on from killing the innocent,
When the thought opposes and goes against inner sense?
My days and nights of a carefree life
Are now stress-filled and overtaken.
I lie at night with a fearful sleep, and I hate when I awaken.

There's no one to run to, no one to talk to.
No comforting arms in this storm while I walk through,

No friends or family, for they've all abandoned.
I've no will to fight, and I'm tired of standing.

No confident thoughts, I'm trapped in my choices.
No one cares for my cries, so I'm left feeling voiceless.
No words to uplift me while feeling my sorrow,
No love for today, and I don't want tomorrow.

So I sit in this park with this gun and this knife,
Choosing the tool with which to take my life.
Too hard a circumstance, no peace, no rest.
Why struggle to find peace? I'll have it in death!
BANG!

— Tareak Johnson

WANTED IN THE KINGDOM OF GOD: THOSE WHO WILL MINISTER TO PREGNANT TEENS

CLASSIFIEDS

VACANCIES NOW STAFFING!

The Kingdom of God seeks persons gifted in the ministry of helps to senior citizens. Must possess excellent interpersonal skills, compassion and patience. Experience a plus. All locations.

Excellent spiritual pay and eternal benefits

CALL: L-O-R-D-S-E-N-D-M-E

* The Kingdom of the Lord Jesus Christ does not discriminate on the basis of race, creed, color, origin or gender.

3

WANTED: Those Who Will Minister to the Lonely

Pure and undefiled religion before God and the Father is this: to visit orphans and widows in their trouble . . .

James 1:27

And then there's old Mrs. Wiggins, her body filled with arthritis, as she peers out of her second-floor window, hoping and praying that today will be different, that today somebody—anybody—will notice that she craves a hug, a wave or even a smile. Then she wouldn't feel so forgotten, so forsaken, so utterly alone.

A Widow's Prayer

Lord, here I am at the window (Thank You for another day)
clothed in my right mind and eyes to see, I pray.
With the pain of arthritis, my body awakes me,
grieving as I rise, for only loneliness awaits me.
Need a little help bathing and tidying up this place,
managed to comb my hair today all by Your grace.

My spouse has passed and my children are grown,
with no time for me in the lives of their own.
I've outlived my siblings; my parents are at rest,
and death has claimed all my friends that were best.
There's no knock at the door or rings of the phone,
no letters in the mail or love in my home.

If I fall to the floor when I'm in pain, will anybody know?
If I call for help when I'm in need, will anybody show?
Through my window, I stay to the world connected
to those who pass by, though I'm totally undetected.
No waves or greetings or smiles on faces,
just distant stares and hurried paces.

Is my life to end like this, all alone in this room?
Send someone to see about me and lift me from this gloom.
Lord, looking back on my life, You've sure been good to me.

And in a few days, by Your grace, I'll celebrate birthday eighty.
Lord, thank You for listening. I know You really care,
and I believe that You'll send someone to answer my prayer.
Amen.

— Tareak Johnson and Linda Gourdine-Hunt

WANTED IN THE KINGDOM OF GOD: Those Who Will Minister to the Lonely

CLASSIFIEDS

ATTENTION!

Seeking full-time and part-time positions for

Mentors

Willing to mentor youth at risk. Must have excellent communication skills and an understanding of teen culture. Knowledge of community resources a plus.

Excellent spiritual pay and eternal benefits

CALL: L-O-R-D-S-E-N-D-M-E

* The Kingdom of the Lord Jesus Christ does not discriminate on the basis of race, creed, color, origin or gender.

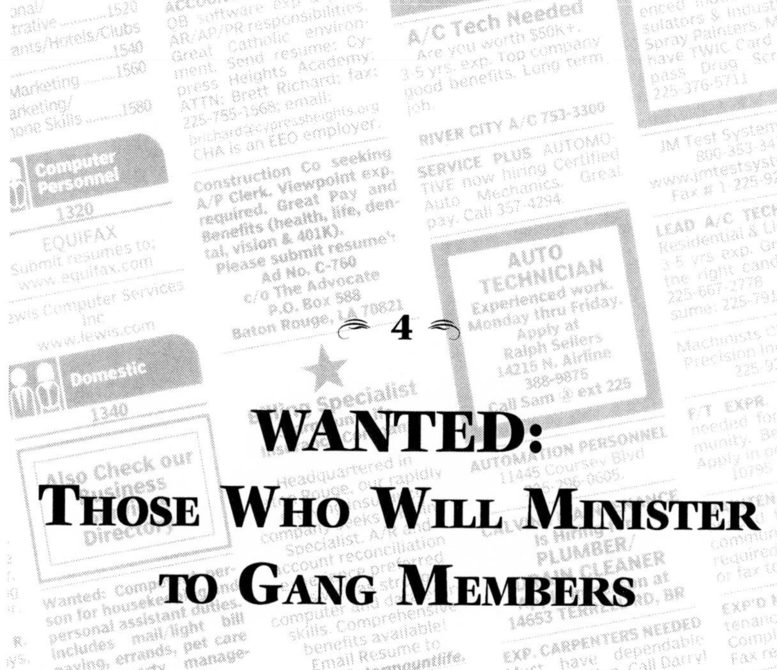

4

WANTED: THOSE WHO WILL MINISTER TO GANG MEMBERS

For we do not wrestle against flesh and blood, but against principalities, against powers, against the rulers of the darkness of this age, against spiritual hosts of wickedness in the heavenly places.

Ephesians 6:12

Pow! Pow! Pow! The sound of gunshots calls our Lord's attention from the west end of the field. There two rival gangs, the Want-It-Nows and the Get-It-Fasts, confront each other and dispute, killing each other over drug territory.

The Case of Kareem

Kareem was only eleven years old when his mother left. She just couldn't take another one of those beatings from her boyfriend.

She had long ago turned to drugs to medicate her wounds and was in and out of prostitution to get her other needs met. And things got really tough for Kareem. She came home less and less ... until she just stopped coming home altogether. Now he had no Mama, no food, no money, no love and no home. He also couldn't bear the beatings anymore. So, Kareem, at eleven, was now on his own and would have to fend for himself in the world.

He slept in abandoned cars, in stairwells and on rooftops—when it wasn't too cold. Sometimes he would go to his friend John's house, just in time for dinner. He longed for what John had: food, a bed, a mom to ask him if he had done his homework, and a dad who would take him out and "kick it" every once in a while.

Known around the neighborhood as "Lil Man," Kareem dropped out of school and began to steal, first for food, then to keep up with the new sneakers that everybody was wearing, and then to support his habits (he had started drinking and smoking marijuana).

Often hiding his tears "cause men don't cry," he yearned for a family. He needed to feel loved and respected and to belong to someone or something. And then the opportunity presented itself. He was recruited into the Gang Bangers. All he had to do for "family" initiation was to participate in a gang rape of a retarded twelve-year-old girl, and he had to go first. For Kareem, violent crime soon became an acceptable and expected way of life.

In June 2006, at the age of 17, Kareem was convicted of rape and manslaughter and was sentenced to ten years in prison. And all he ever wanted was a loving family!

— *Linda Gourdine-Hunt*

(Kareem's story is based on the all-too-true profile of many of the at-risk teens and gang members I have counseled.)

WANTED IN THE KINGDOM OF GOD: Those Who Will Minister to Gang Members

CLASSIFIEDS

VACANCIES

SERVANTS FOR PRISON MINISTRY

Secondary language skills a plus.
Must possess an understanding of family dynamics, a knowledge of community outreach programs and be an intercessory prayer warrior.

All locations

Excellent spiritual pay and eternal benefits

CALL: L-O-R-D-S-E-N-D-M-E

* The Kingdom of the Lord Jesus Christ does not discriminate on the basis of race, creed, color, origin or gender.

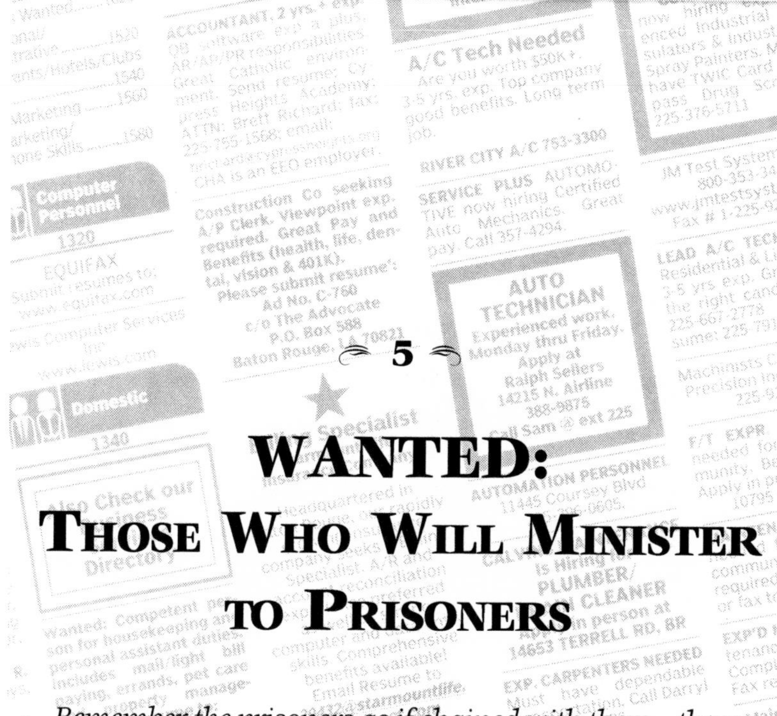

5

WANTED: THOSE WHO WILL MINISTER TO PRISONERS

Remember the prisoners as if chained with them—those who are mistreated—since you yourselves are in the body also. Hebrews 13:3

And I, if I am lifted up from the earth, will draw all peoples to Myself. John 12:32

Up and down the hills our Lord goes, finally arriving on the outskirts of the field. There stands a federal penitentiary filled with men and women. Their faces are pressed hard against the bars of despair. They desperately need a letter, a visit or a call. Seemingly, for them, hope has boarded a space ship and taken a flight into infinity.

Lock Down

Time is tense in this place of consequence,
So keep your back to the fence.
And, when they rush, don't wince.
We have rapes and murders, and insanity grows.
How can this be correction, when your sanity goes?
Some fight and stand strong, while they silently grieve,
Some, weak, become sodomites, to give and receive.
There's no honor amongst thieves,
No love amongst criminals.
Freedom is a state of mind,
while peace of mind is subliminal.
Riots take lives with homemade knives.
Hard times make hard minds and hard hearts inside.
Guards are more crooked than the convicts caged.
The air is thick with the scent of a convict's rage.
Letters become fewer, and phone calls are blocked.
Visitations cease, making it harder on lock.
Teardrops and prayers are commenced at day's end,
From victims of violations committed by crazed men.
Parole is requested in the silence of men's prayers.
Egos dwarf the pain in the hearts of men's cares.
Too hard to show emotion, too tough to express feelings!
Too hurt to let go of the scars to cause healing!

Too guilty to say sorry or even apologize!
Too weak to be strong enough to release our inner cries!
No outside support to relieve the pain, to cope.
Some of us will die from man, others from lack of hope.

— Tareak Johnson

WANTED IN THE KINGDOM OF GOD: Those Who Will Minister to Prisoners

CLASSIFIEDS

VACANCIES

Ministers to the Sick and Shut-In

Willing to nurture and care for the sick and shut-in
and those persons in nursing homes.

Excellent spiritual pay and eternal benefits

CALL: L-O-R-D-S-E-N-D-M-E

* The Kingdom of the Lord Jesus Christ does not discriminate on the basis of race, creed, color, origin or gender.

6

WANTED: THOSE WHO WILL MINISTER TO THE SICK AND SHUT-IN

Is anyone among you suffering? ... Let him call for the elders of the church, and let them pray over him, anointing him with oil in the name of the Lord. And the prayer of faith will save the sick, and the Lord will raise him up. And if he has committed sins, he will be forgiven. James 5:13-15

A busy metropolitan hospital is located up on the east end of the field. The emergency room is jam packed, and on ward after ward, floor after floor, all manner of sickness and disease can be seen. People are hurting, people are crying, and people are even dying. Seeing this, Jesus is moved with compassion.

Where Are You?

Where are you? Where are you? Where are you? You who call yourselves Christians? Guess I've been sick too long.

You started out all right, coming to see me, and then your visits got fewer and fewer ... until they stopped. Where are you? Where are you?

You who are called by His name, why won't you come and pray with me? Can you please go by and see about my children, my mama, my pet? They need some groceries from the store. Where are you? Where are you? I'm afraid! Lord, where's the help?

I need to go to the bathroom, but I can't get up. Lord, please help me!
Won't someone please come and sing a song to ease my pain or rub my fevered brow? Where are you? Where are you?

It would sure lift my spirit to get a call, a card, a visit. I need to hear the Word! Will somebody—anybody—please come and read the Word of God to me? Is this what they mean by "out of sight, out of mind"?

My time will soon be up, and I need you to help me to transition to Glory. Where are you?

Oh yeah, I know where you are:

working ... shopping ... at prayer meeting ...
at the Believers' Luncheon ... going horseback riding
... watching television ... at the salon ... etc.

It's time.
The heavenly angels are here.
I forgive you.

— Linda Gourdine-Hunt

WANTED IN THE KINGDOM OF GOD: THOSE WHO WILL MINISTER TO THE SICK AND SHUT-IN

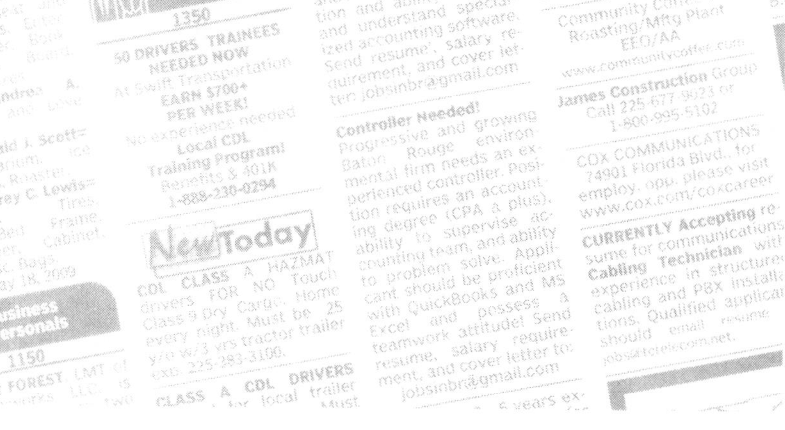

CLASSIFIEDS

VACANCIES

COUNSELORS TO THE CLERGY

Qualifications: Having accepted the Lord Jesus Christ as your personal Savior, having a knowledge of the Word of God, excellent communication skills and a certification in Christian counseling.

All locations.

Excellent spiritual pay and eternal benefits

CALL: L-O-R-D-S-E-N-D-M-E

* The Kingdom of the Lord Jesus Christ does not discriminate on the basis of race, creed, color, origin or gender.

7

WANTED: Those Who Will Minister to Hurting Clergymen

In a multitude of counselors there is safety.

Proverbs 24:6

Around the bend and nestled between two hills stands a steepled church. A quick glance suggests business as usual, but upon closer examination, Jesus finds inside an alcoholic minister, shackled by the chains of embarrassment and depression. You see, this man has severe problems, too, but he feels that he has no one or no place to turn. After all, the people in his congregation surely would not understand.

I'm So Embarrassed

Oh God! I'm so embarrassed! How did this happen to me? How could I be so weak? The anointing is leaving ... No! It's gone! Those who trusted me now laugh at me. I'm a disgrace, a mockery. Help me!

How do I tell them that I don't want to do this anymore? My flesh is weak, and I'm so lonely. Only the bottle is my friend. Lord, I'm just so tired. I wish I had a spouse, someone to share the burden of ministry.

Lord, I love You, but why me? The ministry bills are behind, and I'm now a laughing stock. How can I minister to Your people when I'm in so much pain myself? I'm an alcoholic, and I live in constant fear of being found out.

Time for the pulpit. Here I go, another Sunday morning, me and Johnnie W. getting ready. I gotta get 'em revved up.

I started out all right, didn't I? I really wanted to please You, God, but I didn't know it would be so hard. Then, I just got caught up. After I baptize this baby, say a prayer for Ms. T. and serve Holy Communion, I'm gonna get back in my private place, just me and Johnnie W. I can hardly wait. I'll talk to Johnnie, and everything will be all right. Or will it?

— Linda Gourdine-Hunt

(This profile is based on actual cases of which I am aware)

WANTED IN THE KINGDOM OF GOD: THOSE WHO WILL MINISTER TO HURTING CLERGYMEN

VACANCIES

MISSIONARIES

In all areas of ministry
Immediate hire at home and abroad

Excellent spiritual pay and eternal benefits

CALL: L-O-R-D-S-E-N-D-M-E

* The Kingdom of the Lord Jesus Christ does not discriminate on the basis of race, creed, color, origin or gender.

8

WANTED: Those Who Will Do the Work of Missionaries

For I was hungry and you gave Me food; I was thirsty and you gave Me drink; I was a stranger and you took Me in; I was naked and you clothed Me; I was sick and you visited Me; I was in prison and you came to Me.
Matthew 25:35-36

During visits to Haiti and Africa, I became keenly aware and appreciative of the work of missions everywhere. It's a stark reality that in many Third-World countries, living conditions are severely low. Many people in those nations go hungry, have to exist with substandard housing and face serious health issues. Often their drinking water is contaminated, and there are little or no sanitation facilities, electricity or vital healthcare services. Education is so poor in places that many people remain illiterate. In such conditions, the human spirit is in distress.

While in Africa, I had the heartwrenching experience of watching young children sitting on garbage heaps, seemingly oblivious to the flies and insects crawling on their faces, as their mothers rummaged for their food in the loads of trash left by garbage trucks. Such conditions move the heart of our God and He, in turn, calls us to do what we can to bring change where needed.

Each of us can, in our own way, become a missionary, but the missionaries to the Third-World nations face special challenges.

Hidden Beauty

I sought the Lord with all my heart and soul:
"To whom are You sending me?"

Dressed in a tattered blue skirt and a dingy blouse,
she leaned near the door of the missionary house.
Eating her morning bread, as she watched children play,
she returned, to those who stared, an occasional wave.

Her eyes were filled with a sadness I really couldn't explain,
yet somehow I knew she had seen so much pain.
Her calloused feet shouted the stories of rugged travel,
of a journey where her life had become unraveled.

She was sometimes taunted and sometimes teased,
often alone, ragged and unesteemed.
Longingly staring at others with long braided hair,
she relentlessly scratched at her own, badly in need of care.

And then I knew to whom the Lord had sent me,
for underneath her unkempt exterior there was a hidden beauty.

With a medley of love, skill and compassion,
a godly woman sought those in charge to begin to take action.
The time had come, arrangements were put in place,
to beautify this woman and put a smile on her face.

A young maiden happily volunteers
to wash, oil and twist her matted hair.
But she'd have to wait till the next day to see
just what she truly looks like underneath.
Together we thumbed through pictures in a magazine,
as we awaited her transformation into a beauty queen.

Two young maidens weave extensions
into a beautiful, braided style.
And in only a few hours, it was all worth the while.
For when they were finished and all done with her hair,
we all gathered around and continued to stare.

I handed her a mirror; she gasped in utter disbelief, tearfully expressed gratitude to God in her native Portuguese.
Smiling brightly as the noonday sun,
she began posing and taking pictures for everyone.

On my last day, as I got ready to leave,
stood the queen near the door in radiant glory.
"Thank you very much," in English she uttered,
with a genuine heart of gratitude, witnessed by me and others.
My heart was filled with joy, for the mission was done.
Sometimes Jesus sends us to the masses; other times just to one.

— Linda Gourdine-Hunt

WANTED IN THE KINGDOM OF GOD: THOSE WHO WILL DO THE WORK OF MISSIONARIES

CLASSIFIEDS

HELP WANTED!

POSITIONS:

FIELD HANDS

Duties (including, but not limited to): Preaching the Gospel, casting out demons, laying hands on the sick, feeding the hungry, clothing the naked, sheltering the homeless, comforting those who mourn, hugging someone, shaking a hand, waving, smiling, reaching out, speaking an encouraging word. Making a difference!

* The Kingdom of the Lord Jesus Christ does not discriminate on the basis of race, creed, color, origin or gender.

9

The Call Goes Forth

But when He saw the multitudes, He was moved with compassion for them, because they were weary and scattered, like sheep having no shepherd. Then He said to His disciples, "The harvest truly is plentiful, but the laborers are few. Therefore pray the Lord of the harvest to send out laborers into His harvest."

Matthew 9:36-38

Everywhere Jesus goes He encounters the pain and sufferings of His people. He is moved with compassion for them, because they are harassed, distressed, dejected and helpless, like sheep without a shepherd.

So, on His way back to Glory, He decides to send out an urgent call to those who are called by His name, and it reads like the poster on the opposite page.

Who is our Lord calling? If you are one of His, then *you* are included in this call. Hear His voice today.

And, please, answer the call.

WANTED IN THE KINGDOM OF GOD:

THOSE WHO WILL BE THE HANDS, FEET AND MOUTH OF OUR LORD JESUS CHRIST TO DEMONSTRATE HIS LOVE TO A HURTING WORLD

Part II

Answering the Call

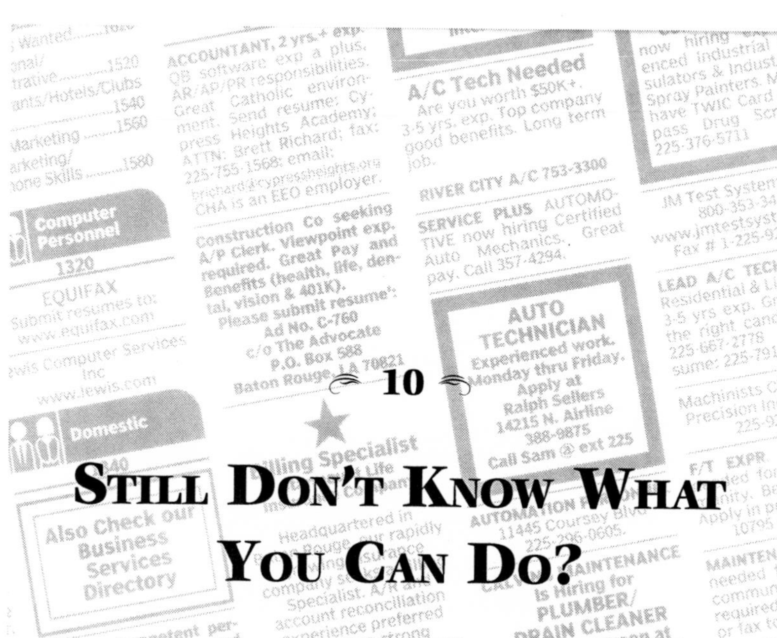

10

Still Don't Know What You Can Do?

Do unto others as you would have them do unto you.

The Golden Rule

How God anointed Jesus of Nazareth with the Holy Spirit and with power, who went about doing good and healing all who were oppressed by the devil, for God was with Him.

Acts 10:38

If you still don't know exactly what you might do in the Kingdom of God, here are a few suggestions:

For Yourself

- Laugh
- Reserve some quiet time for yourself
- Take classes in an area of interest or need
- Learn a new trade

- Take time to enjoy nature
- Take time to get adequate and proper rest
- Learn to speak another language
- Be a friend to others
- Be a peacemaker
- Be forgiving
- Be encouraging
- Be excited about the Gospel of Jesus Christ
- Be kind
- Be an excellent employee
- Be an excellent employer
- Get regular health checkups, dental and eye care
- Foster good friendships and associations
- Acknowledge those who do good to you

IN THE CHURCH SETTING

- Counsel others
- Join a ministry in your local church
- Get actively involved in support of some ministry
- Advertise and/or market Christian products
- Design a Christian web page
- Visit the sick
- Start a group for young mothers
- Start a book club
- Do creative arts
- Donate your good used clothing to help others
- Teach Sunday school
- Mentor a child
- Give scholarships to deserving youth

At Home

- Celebrate special occasions
- Play games and have fun
- Rake the yard
- Plan recreational activities
- Learn to recycle
- Express thanks and gratitude to other family members on a daily basis
- Spend quality time with your family
- Manage your finances wisely
- Help with the household chores
- Help to care for family pets
- Organize a family reunion
- Plant flowers and otherwise beautify your surroundings

In the Community

- Coach a team
- Sing in community programs
- Join a community agency
- Help clean and beautify your community
- Advocate for services within your community
- Do volunteer work in a hospital or other public-service agency
- Walk for the cure of a disease
- Donate your good used clothing to those less fortunate
- Collect and distribute food for the needy
- Visit a nursing home
- Plant a garden
- Teach a child to read

- Share your testimony
- Sponsor a needy child
- Provide workshops/classes on topics of interest
- Start a support group for an addictive behavior
- Write articles for a local publication
- Become an advocate for issues that are opposed to the teachings of God's Holy Word such as abortion and same-sex marriage.
- Baby-sit for a neighbor
- Shop for someone
- Prepare a meal for someone
- Offer someone a ride
- Extend hospitality to someone in need
- Sew for someone
- Bake a cake for someone
- Do needed gardening for someone
- Paint for someone
- Draw an encouraging picture for someone
- Treat someone to a movie
- Send someone a greeting card
- Hire someone in need of employment
- Tell someone the Good News of the Gospel
- Use your gifts and talents in the service of others and, in this way, extend the Kingdom of God

* The Kingdom of the Lord Jesus Christ does not discriminate on the basis of race, creed, color, origin or gender.

11

Preparation for Service

But we will give ourselves continually to prayer and to the ministry of the word. Acts 6:4

If you have felt the call of God on your life to serve Him in any capacity, then the next step you need to take is to prepare yourself for service. Here are some scriptures that can help you do that.

Preparation through Prayer

Blessed be God,
Who has not turned away my prayer,
Nor His mercy from me! Psalm 66:20

And whatever things you ask in prayer, believing, you will receive. Matthew 21:22

Rejoicing in hope, patient in tribulation, continuing steadfastly in prayer. Romans 12:12

I exhort first of all that supplications, prayers, intercessions, and giving of thanks be made for all men.
1 Timothy 2:1

But the end of all things is at hand; therefore be serious and watchful in your prayers. 1 Peter 4:7

Continue earnestly in prayer, being vigilant in it with thanksgiving. Colossians 4:2

PREPARATION THROUGH FASTING

Moreover, when you fast, do not be like the hypocrites, with a sad countenance. For they disfigure their faces that they may appear to men to be fasting. Assuredly, I say to you, they have their reward. Matthew 6:16

PREPARATION THROUGH THE STUDY OF THE WORD OF GOD

Be diligent to present yourself approved to God, a worker who does not need to be ashamed, rightly dividing the word of truth. 2 Timothy 2:15

If then you were raised with Christ, seek those things which are above, where Christ is, sitting at the right hand of God. Colossians 3:1

Jesus answered and said to them, "You are mistaken, not knowing the Scriptures nor the power of God."
Matthew 22:29

You search the Scriptures, for in them you think you have eternal life; and these are they which testify of Me. John 5:39

All Scripture is given by inspiration of God, and is profitable for doctrine, for reproof, for correction, for instruction in righteousness, that the man of God may be complete, thoroughly equipped for every good work.
2 Timothy 3:16-17

Preparation through Meditation on the Word

Oh, how I love Your law!
It is my meditation all the day. Psalm 119:97

I will meditate on Your precepts,
And contemplate Your ways. Psalm 119:15

This Book of the Law shall not depart from your mouth, but you shall meditate in it day and night, that you may observe to do according to all that is written in it. For then you will make your way prosperous, and then you will have good success. Joshua 1:8

My hands also I will lift up to Your commandments,
Which I love,
And I will meditate on Your statutes. Psalm 119:48

Finally, brethren, whatever things are true, whatever

things are noble, whatever things are just, whatever things are pure, whatever things are lovely, whatever things are of good report, if there is any virtue and if there is anything praiseworthy—meditate on these things. Philippians 4:8

Preparation through Attending Anointed Services

Not forsaking the assembling of ourselves together, as is the manner of some, but exhorting one another, and so much the more as you see the Day approaching.

Hebrews 10:25

From whom the whole body, joined and knit together by what every joint supplies, according to the effective working by which every part does its share, causes growth of the body for the edifying of itself in love.

Ephesians 4:16

Preparation through The Giving of Your Resources

Honor the Lord with your possessions,
And with the firstfruits of all your increase.

Proverbs 3:9

So let each one give as he purposes in his heart, not grudgingly or of necessity; for God loves a cheerful giver.

2 Corinthians 9:7

Preparation through Regular Health Checkups

Beloved, I pray that you may prosper in all things and be in health, just as your soul prospers. 3 John 1:2

Jesus answered and said to them, "Those who are well have no need of a physician, but those who are sick." Luke 5:31

But to you who fear My name
The Sun of Righteousness shall arise
With healing in His wings;
And you shall go out
And grow fat like stall-fed calves. Malachi 4:2

Or do you not know that your body is the temple of the Holy Spirit who is in you, whom you have from God, and you are not your own? For you were bought at a price; therefore glorify God in your body and in your spirit, which are God's. 1 Corinthians 6:19-20

Preparation through Getting Proper Nutrition

And God said, "See, I have given you every herb that yields seed which is on the face of all the earth, and every tree whose fruit yields seed; to you it shall be for food. Genesis 1:29

When you sit down to eat ... ,
Consider carefully what is before you. Proverbs 23:1

When you eat the labor of your hands,
You shall be happy, and it shall be well with you.
Psalm 128:2

PREPARATION THROUGH GETTING PROPER EXERCISE

I beseech you therefore, brethren, by the mercies of God, that ye present your bodies a living sacrifice, holy, acceptable unto God, which is your reasonable service.
Romans 12:1, KLV

Wherefore we labour, that, whether present or absent, we may be accepted of him. 2 Corinthians 5:9, KJV

Therefore, my beloved brethren, be steadfast, immovable, always abounding in the work of the Lord, knowing that your labor is not in vain in the Lord.
1 Corinthians 15:58

To this end I also labor, striving according to His working which works in me mightily. Colossians 1:29

PREPARATION THROUGH GETTING PROPER REST

Let us labour therefore to enter into that rest, lest any man fall after the same example of unbelief. Hebrews 4:11, KLV

Come to Me, all you who labor and are heavy laden, and I will give you rest. Take My yoke upon you and learn from Me, for I am gentle and lowly in heart, and you will find rest for your souls. Matthew 11:28-29

Rest in the Lord, *and wait patiently for Him;*
Do not fret because of him who prospers in his way,
Because of the man who brings wicked schemes to pass.

Psalm 37:7

Preparation through Continuously Developing New Skills

And they continued steadfastly in the apostles' doctrine and fellowship, in the breaking of bread, and in prayers.

Acts 2:42

Therefore, my beloved brethren, be steadfast, immovable, always abounding in the work of the Lord, knowing that your labor is not in vain in the Lord.

1 Corinthians 15:58

But also for this very reason, giving all diligence, add to your faith virtue, to virtue knowledge, to knowledge self-control, to self-control perseverance, to perseverance godliness, to godliness brotherly kindness, and to brotherly kindness love. For if these things are yours and abound, you will be neither barren nor unfruitful in the knowledge of our Lord Jesus Christ.

2 Peter 1:5-8

But seek first the kingdom of God and His righteousness, and all these things shall be added to you.

Matthew 6:33

Therefore, brethren, be even more diligent to make your call and election sure, for if you do these things you will never stumble. 2 Peter 1:10

As you are faithful to prepare yourself for service, the call of God will become more clear to you and you will become more fruitful for God's Kingdom.

* The Kingdom of the Lord Jesus Christ does not discriminate on the basis of race, creed, color, origin or gender.

12

What Our Youth Want to See

Where there is no vision, the people perish.

Proverbs 29:18, KJV

I asked a group of young people what they thought was needed in the Kingdom of God today. Here are some of their most interesting responses:

- More advertisement of ministries for young people
- A better presentation of the youth to others (many times we are seen in a negative way, and we need more positive things to be said about us)
- More creative ways of teaching God's Word, such as drama
- Doing more fun things with the youth of the church, things like bowling and going on trips
- Having access to more godly men who could help us to make wiser decisions

One young lady responded: "I was a teenage mom, and I wanted to go to church, but every time I went I was made to feel bad because of what I had done. Teenage moms need a church where they can go and feel loved and get help—even though they have 'messed up.' "

Let the heartcry of these young people speak to you today.

* The Kingdom of the Lord Jesus Christ does not discriminate on the basis of race, creed, color, origin or gender.

13

OTHERS SHARE

For the body is not one member, but many.

1 Corinthians 12:14, KJV

I asked other friends and family members to share their thoughts here, and some did. Here is the result:

Needed

Needed: parents who are eager to learn of and experience the love of our Father and develop a personal relationship with Him and willing to open their minds and hearts to accept and apply the wisdom of the ages to their lives and the lives of their children.
Needed: parents who are teachable and, therefore, open to learning themselves.

Needed: parents who know and understand that they, like all peoples of the world, are wondrously made for

God's pleasure, and who find fulfilment in being examples of respect, kindness, justice and love.
Needed: parents who, by example, will teach and pass down to their children the power of the Word of God and of prayer.

Needed: parents who are not so preoccupied that they forget to pause, stop and meditate on the awesome sovereignty of the One who formed the earth, covered the sky with stars, set in place seas and oceans, beautified the plains and valleys with flowers and animals, carved majestic mountains, and mixed the perfect colors for the trees of the forests in order to refresh our spirits and serve as a constant reminder to worship and praise Him.

Needed: parents who will teach their children, who, in turn, will teach their *children, and on and on it will go.*

— Katherine McIver

Men Wanted!

For we who call ourselves men,
let's strive to be present in our families from beginning to end.
We profess to love our children, whom we helped procreate,
so when it comes to our responsibility, let's not deviate.

We boast about being the head of our households,

yet, too often our women must pick up the pieces,
because we become weak and fold.
And when we look in our churches at leadership roles,
women, by far, carry the torch, let the truth be told.

So where are you good men? I dare to ask.
Step up. Step forward and take on the task.
For God has designed us to be at the helm.
Let's seek Him first so we won't be overwhelmed.

While developing our masculinity, we strive to build up muscle,
but when strength really matters, let's look to God
to help us through the struggle.

Break down the barriers. Let down our macho shields.
God is calling men to work in the fields!

— Steve Hunt

Why?

God, in His grace, has allowed seniors to live the promise, and yet we are sometimes forsaken and downtrodden by many.
We say we love God, who we've never seen, but we cast aside our brothers and sisters whom we live among daily.
I am a woman of eighty and a half years whom God has truly blessed, and I am also a widow.
In the earlier years of life, we were in a position to

help bridge the gap to bring us into the present. In the eyes of the Father, I do feel special love, because His Word says, "You shall not afflict any widow or fatherless child. If you afflict them in any way, and they cry at all to Me, I will surely hear their cry" (*Exodus 22:22-23*).

In John 13:34, God has said, "A new commandment I give to you, that you love one another; as I have loved you, that you also love one another." *The elderly and widow should never desire to be a burden, but just want to be a part of the Body.*

This message is not to judge or criticize but only to awaken the Body to be obedient to the Word of God, which says: "Till we all come to the unity of the faith and of the knowledge of the Son of God, to a perfect man, to the measure of the stature of the fullness of Christ" (*Ephesians 4:13*).

I hope and pray that this message will help us to respond and unite in the call that our Father has placed upon us.

Let us please our Father. It is not about us; it's all about Him.

— Anonymous

Help Take the Limits Off

Help! Help! Help us! Not just across the street, but to the throne where Jesus sits.

Why do people discriminate? Why do people think that because we are blind or visually impaired God has forgotten us? Why don't they realize that He's manifesting His glory through us? If the Lord has allowed us to go through this, it must mean that He's equipped us to handle it.

In the church, we are encouraged to pray and seek the Lord for the ministry He wants to use us in, but when we say something like "children's ministry" or "street ministry," we, the blind and visually impaired, are often judged by our physical eyes and not our spiritual eyes, and therefore limits are placed upon us. When people do this, they may not realize it, but they are putting limits on God. Is God not able? If He gave us the assignment, that means He's anointed us to serve with excellence.

Remember, there's no darkness in Jesus. He sees very well, and He's not confused about His vision for His Kingdom. Acts 10:34 tells us that God doesn't discriminate. He also has said that all Christians are equal in His eyes, and don't forget what He said in Colossians 3:25. He will judge those who discriminate.

So please, take the limits off of God.

— Tonya Hunt

WANTED: Merciful Christians

Christians are saved by grace, grace that is afforded to the underserving. *"It is the gift of God, not of works, lest anyone should boast"* (Ephesians 2:8-9). We are fellow members of the household of God. As members of God's family, we are obligated to be forgiving and merciful to others. Ephesians 4:32 tells us: *"be kind to one another, tenderhearted, forgiving one another, even as God in Christ forgave you."*

Too often we find "Christians" who have been hardened by their past and hindered by their present experiences, but God's grace is sufficient. As ambassadors of Christ, we are to set our minds on things above, not on things on the earth. Conflicts, insecurity and worry may cause us to lose sight of who we are in Christ, and the concerns of the world can affect our relationships within the Body of Christ.

Wanted: Merciful Christians who can remember that we are God's workmanship. *"Therefore, as the elect of God, holy and beloved, put on tender mercies, kindness, humility, meekness, longsuffering; bearing with one another. If anyone has a complaint against another; even as Christ forgave you, so you also must do" (Colossians* 3:12-13).

On this day, are you willing to forgive those who have caused you pain? Will you answer the call for mercy?

— *Brenda Williams*

* The Kingdom of the Lord Jesus Christ does not discriminate on the basis of race, creed, color, origin or gender.

14

The Role of Prayer in All Ministries

Therefore I exhort first of all that supplications, prayers, intercessions, and giving of thanks be made for all men.

1 Timothy 2:1

Since every ministry emanates from the heart of God, it must begin in prayer and continue in prayer. In the sacred Scriptures we are taught to pray for the following:

Pray for Secular Leaders

Therefore, I exhort first of all that supplications, prayers, intercessions, and giving of thanks be made for all men, for kings and all who are in authority, that we may lead a quiet and peaceable life in all godliness and reverence.

1 Timothy 2:1-2

Pray for the Peace of Jerusalem

Pray for the peace of Jerusalem:
May they prosper who love you. Psalm 122:6

Pray for Our Children

Now therefore, listen to me, my children,
For blessed are those who keep my ways.
Proverbs 8:32

Arise, cry out in the night,
At the beginning of the watches;
Pour out your heart like water before the face of the LORD.
Lift your hands toward Him
For the life of your young children,
Who faint from hunger at the head of every street.
Lamentations 2:19

Pray for a Cure for Diseases

So you shall serve the LORD *your God, and He will bless your bread and your water. And I will take sickness away from the midst of you.* Exodus 23:25

Pray for Employment

And my God shall supply all your need according to His riches in glory by Christ Jesus. Philippians 4:19

Pray for Pastors and Other Ministers

The Spirit of the Lord God is upon Me,
Because the Lord has anointed Me
To preach good tidings to the poor;
He has sent Me to heal the brokenhearted,
To proclaim liberty to the captives,
And the opening of the prison to those who are bound.

Isaiah 61:1

Pray for the Sick and Shut-Ins

And the prayer of faith will save the sick, and the Lord will raise him up. And if he has committed sins, he will be forgiven. James 5:15

Pray for the Mentally Infirm

For God has not given us a spirit of fear, but of power and of love and of a sound mind.

2 Timothy 1:7

Pray for the Spreading of the Gospel of Jesus Christ

And He said to them, "Go into all the world and preach the gospel to every creature." Mark 16:15

Pray for the Bereaved

Blessed are those who mourn,

For they shall be comforted. Matthew 5:4

PRAY FOR THOSE WHO HAVE ADDICTIONS

Stand fast therefore in the liberty by which Christ has made us free, and do not be entangled again with a yoke of bondage. Galatians 5:1

PRAY FOR THOSE WHO ARE BOUND BY SIN

If we confess our sins, He is faithful and just to forgive us our sins and to cleanse us from all unrighteousness. 1 John 1:9

PRAY FOR TROUBLED MARRIAGES

So then, they are no longer two but one flesh. Therefore what God has joined together, let not man separate. Matthew 19:6

PRAY FOR A HEALTHY ECONOMY

For I do not mean that others should be eased and you burdened; but by an equality, that now at this time your abundance may supply their lack, that their abundance also may supply your lack—that there may be equality. As it is written, "He who gathered much had nothing left over, and he who gathered little had no lack." 2 Corinthians 8:13-15

Pray for those Impacted by Natural Disasters

If My people who are called by My name will humble themselves, and pray and seek My face, and turn from their wicked ways, then I will hear from heaven, and will forgive their sin and heal their land.

2 Chronicles 7:14

Pray for Growth and Development among Believers

But also for this very reason, giving all diligence, add to your faith virtue, to virtue knowledge, to knowledge self-control, to self-control perseverance, to perseverance godliness, to godliness brotherly kindness, and to brotherly kindness love. For if these things are yours and abound, you will be neither barren nor unfruitful in the knowledge of our Lord Jesus Christ. 2 Peter 1:5-8

Pray for Missionaries on Foreign Soil

And He said to them, "Go into all the world and preach the gospel to every creature." Mark 16:15

Pray for the Care and Preservation for Our Natural Resources

The earth is the Lord's, *and all its fullness,*
The world and those who dwell therein. Psalm 24:1

PRAY FOR THOSE WHO DO NOT KNOW CHRIST

Draw near to God and He will draw near to you. Cleanse your hands, you sinners; and purify your hearts, you double-minded. James 4:8

PRAY FOR THE HOMELESS

For the poor will never cease from the land; therefore I command you, saying, "You shall open your hand wide to your brother, to your poor and your needy, in your land." Deuteronomy 15:11

This poor man cried out, and the LORD heard him, And saved him out of all his troubles. Psalm 34:6

PRAY FOR THE VICTIMS OF CHILD PORNOGRAPHY AND PROSTITUTION

Flee also youthful lusts; but pursue righteousness, faith, love, peace with those who call on the Lord out of a pure heart. 2 Timothy 2:22

PRAY FOR IMPROVEMENTS IN OUR EDUCATIONAL SYSTEM

If My people who are called by My name will humble themselves, and pray and seek My face, and turn from their wicked ways, then I will hear from heaven, and will forgive their sin and heal their land.

2 Chronicles 7:14

For the LORD gives wisdom;
From His mouth come knowledge and understanding.

Proverbs 2:6

PRAY FOR SINGLE MOTHERS AND FATHERS

Train up a child in the way he should go,
And when he is old he will not depart from it.

Proverbs 22:6

As you make prayer more and more a part of your everyday life, you will become more fruitful for the Kingdom of God.

* The Kingdom of the Lord Jesus Christ does not discriminate on the basis of race, creed, color, origin or gender.

Appendices

* The Kingdom of the Lord Jesus Christ does not discriminate on the basis of race, creed, color, origin or gender.

AN INVITATION TO CHRIST

Jesus said to him, "I am the way, the truth, and the life. No one comes to the Father except through Me."
John 14:6

Paul wrote to the Romans:

If you confess with your mouth the Lord Jesus and believe in your heart that God has raised Him from the dead, you will be saved. For with the heart one believes unto righteousness, and with the mouth confession is made unto salvation. Romans 10:9-10

Here's how you can receive Christ as your Lord and Savior right this moment:

1. Admit that you are a sinner. (See Romans 3:10)
2. Repent (turn from sin) (See Acts 17:30)
3. Believe that Jesus Christ died for you, was buried and rose from the dead. (See Romans 10:9-10)
4. Invite Jesus into your life to become your personal Saviour. (See Romans 10:13)

If you don't know what to pray, you might want to say a prayer like this:

Dear God,
I am a sinner. Forgive me of my sin. I believe that Jesus Christ shed His precious blood and died to save

me. I now invite Christ to come into my heart and life as my personal Savior.

If you prayed that prayer, then welcome into the family of God. You are now a new creature in Christ:

Therefore, if anyone is in Christ, he is a new creation; old things have passed away; behold, all things have become new. 2 Corinthians 5:17

Ask God to lead you to a church where Christ is preached and the Bible (the Word of God) is the highest and final authority. Be faithful to that church so that you can grow in grace and develop the special talents and abilities God has placed within you. And be sure to seek your special place of service in God's Kingdom. He has something unique and exciting for you to do for Him.

* The Kingdom of the Lord Jesus Christ does not discriminate on the basis of race, creed, color, origin or gender.

An Application for Employment in The Kingdom of God

Your name: ______________________________ Date: _______

Have you accepted Jesus Christ as your personal Savior and Lord? Yes ❑ No ❑

Please state your motivation for service:

____

____

In what area/s of ministry has God called you?

____

____

What are your skills, talent/s and gifts?

____

____

____

Days of availability: ____________________________

Hours of availability: ____________________________

Previous experience: ____________________________

Are you willing to give God all the glory for the things He does through you? Yes ❑ No ❑

CALL: L-O-R-D-S-E-N-D-M-E

Then Jesus went about all the cities and villages, teaching in their synagogues, preaching the gospel of the kingdom, and healing every sickness and every disease among the people. But when He saw the multitudes, He was moved with compassion for them, because they were weary and scattered, like sheep having no shepherd. Then He said to His disciples, "The harvest truly is plentiful, but the laborers are few. Therefore pray the Lord of the harvest to send out laborers into His harvest." Matthew 9:35-38

Notes

Notes

Notes

Notes

MINISTRY PAGE

You may reach the author at the following addresses:

Linda Gourdine-Hunt
Divine Inspirations Messenger
P.O. Box 340407
Rochdale Village, NY 11434

email: lindaagh3@aol.com

Breinigsville, PA USA
11 January 2010
230474BV00001B/4/P